HOT TOPICS

HUMAN RIGHTS

Mark Friedman

Heinemann
LIBRARY
Chicago, Illinois

www.capstonepub.com
Visit our website to find out more information about Heinemann-Raintree books.

To order:
☎ Phone 888-454-2279
💻 Visit www.capstonepub.com
   to browse our catalog and order online.

Edited by Adam Miller, Nick Hunter, and
 Diyan Leake
Designed by Philippa Jenkins
Original illustrations © Capstone Global
 Library Ltd 2012
Picture research by Mica Brancic
Production by Eirian Griffiths and Alison Parsons
Originated by Capstone Global Library Ltd
Printed and bound in the USA by Corporate Graphics

15 14 13 12 11
10 9 8 7 6 5 4 3 2 1

Library of Congress Cataloging-in-Publication Data
Friedman, Mark, 1963-
  Human rights / Mark Friedman.
     p. cm.—(Hot topics)
  Includes bibliographical references and index.
  ISBN 978-1-4329-6035-3 (hb)—ISBN 978-1-4329-6043-8 (pb) 1. Human rights. I. Title.
  JC571.F694 2012
  323—dc23   2011023103

Acknowledgments
The author and publisher are grateful to the following for permission to reproduce copyright material: Alamy pp. 45 (© Penny Tweedie), 54 (© Hemis/Christophe Boisvieux); Corbis pp. 4 (Sygma/ © Jose Nicolas), 7 (© Heritage Images), 10 (© Stefano Bianchetti), 14, 18 (Sygma/© Bernard Bisson), 21 (© Reuters/Goran Tomasevic), 23 (epa/© Abedin Taherkenareh), 25 (© Ted Soqui), 27 (epa/© Nyein Chan Naing), 31 (epa/© Abir Abdullah), 34 (epa/© Nic Bothma), 35 (© David Brabyn), 37 (epa/© Jawad Jalali), 43 (Reuters/ © Ulli Michel), 51 (Reuters/ X00226/© Romeo Ranoco), 57 (Reuters/Arthur Tsang); Getty Images pp. 12 (Archive Photos/ Fotosearch), 16 (AFP Photo/Yuriy Dyachyshyn), 39 (Warrick Page), 41 (Hulton Archive/Keystone), 53 (NY Daily News Archive/Todd Maisel); Press Association pp. 28 (Petr David Josek), 33 (Shehzad Noorani); Shutterstock p. 47 (© Lizette Potgieter).

Cover photograph of supporters of migrant workers on the US–Mexico border, behind a fence in Los Angeles, California, USA on 21 May 2006, reproduced with permission of Corbis (Reuters/ X01783/© Lucas Jackson).

Every effort has been made to contact copyright holders of material reproduced in this book. Any omissions will be rectified in subsequent printings if notice is given to the publishers.

CONTENTS

Some words are printed in bold, **like this**. You can find out what they mean by looking in the glossary.

THE STRUGGLE FOR HUMAN RIGHTS

Working in a gravel pit is difficult. Crushing huge stones into tiny pieces of gravel is physically demanding and potentially dangerous. To make gravel properly, you need heavy machinery to dig the boulders out of the ground, crush the stone into smaller pieces, and haul the gravel. You need to wear protective clothing so that you will not get injured or inhale the harmful dust that crushing the stone can produce. If you are treated fairly, you have access to a good healthcare so that, if you do get sick or injured on the job, you can receive medical treatment.

■ This young gravel-pit worker spends her days crushing rocks.

However, a quarry worker named Alone Banda, in the African country of Zambia, had none of these things. Even worse, Alone Banda was a 9-year-old boy doing this work. Adult workers would break the big boulders down to smaller rocks. They would then sell those rocks to child workers such as Alone, who would use hammers to beat the gravel into powder. They would then sell bags of the crushed rock to construction companies, which use the materials in mixing concrete.

Alone did not have a choice. He could not leave this job and spend more time in school. If he had left, he would starve. Alone and his grandmother lived together in a filthy, one-room house. Alone slept on the floor. The money he made was usually just enough to provide them with food to eat. But sometimes, there was not enough to eat, or time to eat. Alone worked long hours. "I break the rocks. I get up early in the morning, before the sun rises. For breakfast, I drink tea sometimes. This morning, I didn't eat. I'm hungry," he said.

What are human rights?

You might think that Alone's experience happened a long time ago. But around the world today, thousands of children like Alone continue to perform dangerous work to avoid starvation. Children and adults are mistreated in many other ways as well. For example, people are punished for speaking out against their government; people are held in prison without having their cases tried in courts; and people are actually murdered by their own leaders or governments. Tragedies such as these are all **violations** of human rights. Human rights are rights that are held by all human beings. They include the rights to:

- life, liberty, and the pursuit of happiness
- equal treatment
- own property
- practice religion.

You will explore many human rights in this book. The common trait of all these rights is that they belong to everyone. Just as humans are born with a brain, a heart, a certain color of eyes and hair, and other physical qualities, we are also born with rights. It is almost as if these rights are part of nature. Just as it would be wrong to try to take away someone's brain, it is also wrong to try to take away someone's human rights. No matter what country people live in, they have human rights. No matter how much money people earn, they have human rights. No matter what race or ethnic group or gender people belong to, they have human rights.

Who violates human rights?

Most people who live in **democratic** societies, such as the United Kingdom and the United States, expect human rights to be automatic. We think of our human rights as guaranteed. In fact, there is a written guarantee of those rights. Most democratic nations' **constitutions** or other legal documents make sure that the basic human rights of each citizen are protected by the government. If those rights are violated, the government must find and punish the criminals. Protecting its citizens is one of the main jobs of a government.

If you are mugged or beaten up, it is obvious that your rights have been violated by another person. But these are crimes committed by individuals against other individuals. When we talk about human rights violations, we are talking about the government or other leaders committing crimes against the citizens they are supposed to be protecting. We could also be discussing large corporations that use the power of their size and wealth to commit human rights violations. Human rights crimes occur when governments or other leaders stop women from wearing the clothing they want to wear, or keep citizens in a state of starvation, or go as far as attacking or even murdering citizens.

Natural rights and human rights

The discussion about natural rights goes back thousands of years to the ancient Greeks and Romans. In those civilizations, philosophers determined that laws were not handed down by gods. Instead, laws existed as part of nature. So each individual person automatically has rights as part of nature, not because of someone's, or some god's, decision.

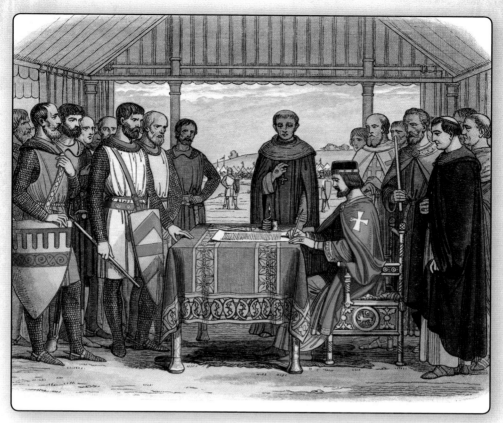
■ This 19th-century engraving shows King John signing the Magna Carta in 1215.

Throughout the centuries, the idea of natural rights has been discussed by many thinkers and rulers. Many civilizations were built on the idea that slavery was permissible and that certain classes of people were lower than others. Therefore, lower classes of people did not have the same rights as others. Gradually, societies changed, and more human rights were recognized. In 1215, the Magna Carta was signed in England. This document put limits on the powers of the king and stated that individuals have certain rights. For instance, the Magna Carta stated that people are free and that no free person can be imprisoned unless they are convicted in a fair trial. In generations to come, other governments would base their constitutions on the ideas set forth in the Magna Carta.

Hobbes and Locke

As time passed, governments and great thinkers continued to develop ideas about natural rights. Thomas Hobbes (1588–1679) wrote a book in 1651 called *Leviathan*, in which he promoted the idea that governments are necessary to stop **chaos** from destroying societies. Since every individual has natural freedoms, we would be at war with each other unless there were laws that governed society.

Hobbes believed that all men are naturally equals. John Locke (1632–1704) took this thinking several steps further. He wrote that all men have the rights to life, liberty, and property. This meant that once people are born, they have the right to live their life without anyone else interfering with them. The right to liberty means that people should be able to do whatever they want to do as long as they don't interfere with the liberty of others. And the right to property means that people should be able to keep the money or property that they earn.

WHAT DO YOU THINK?

Thomas Jefferson was one of those who signed the United States Declaration of Independence and was the main author of the Constitution. But like many other men in 18th-century America, Jefferson owned slaves. As a slave-owner, Jefferson denied these people the same rights that the Revolution had fought to win for other Americans. But at the time, the farm-based American society relied on slaves for manual labor. Jefferson is known to have hated the idea of slavery, but he realized that freeing all slaves would be disastrous for the American economy.

Do *you* think Jefferson should have freed his slaves?

Revolutions for rights

The writings of these and other thinkers led to action. In the 1700s, two major **revolutions** took place. Both were based on the rights of individuals. In North America, the American colonists (British settlers) broke away from Great Britain when they signed the Declaration of Independence in 1776 and started the Revolutionary War. There were many reasons for the war, but one of the main causes was taxes. People in the colonies did not want to pay taxes to the British king without being represented in the British **parliament**. The colonists believed that the money they earned should remain in the colonies, and, if they were to pay taxes, they should be able to represent themselves in the government that was taxing them.

The ideas behind this thinking go back to John Locke and the rights that he laid out. Individuals have the rights to life, liberty, and property, and the colonists believed that Great Britain was denying them those rights. The Americans went to war to win their independence from Britain. The Revolutionary War lasted from 1775 to 1783 and established the United States of America. After the war ended, leaders of the new nation wrote the Bill of Rights in 1789. Much of the thinking by Locke and other past writings on natural rights influenced the Bill of Rights. The new American document set forth all of the ways in which individuals' rights must be protected by the government. It also set limits on the powers held by government.

> "We hold these truths to be self-evident, that all men are created equal, that they are endowed by their Creator with certain unalienable Rights, that among these are Life, Liberty and the pursuit of Happiness."
>
> **The United States Declaration of Independence**

Almost at the same time as the American Revolution ended, the French Revolution was about to begin. Citizens in France wrote the Declaration of the Rights of Man and of the Citizen in 1789. This document declared many of the same types of individual rights that the Americans had claimed. In 1789, the people of France went to the streets in a violent revolt against the monarchy. The revolution ended ten years later, when a new constitution was signed that guaranteed rights to all citizens.

■ The Storming of the Bastille in 1789—the battle that sparked the French Revolution.

The birth of the modern human rights movement

In the two centuries that followed these landmark revolutions, democracy spread to many countries around the world, making it possible for more people to enjoy human rights. Democracies are not perfect, however, and some democracies were established while certain groups were still denied their human rights. For instance, in the United States, African Americans did not achieve equal rights until nearly two centuries after the Constitution and Bill of Rights were established.

At the same time, many countries did not embrace democracy. Human rights often suffered in those places. Throughout the 20th century, many nations were ruled by strict governments that denied many human rights to their citizens. Countries such as China, the **Soviet Union** (which later broke up into Russia and other countries), Germany, Italy, and Spain were controlled by all-powerful **dictators** at some point during the last century. These dictators inflicted harsh treatment on their citizens. During World War II (1939–1945), Adolf Hitler led Germany in one of the largest slaughters of innocent human life in history. Hitler's **Holocaust** against the Jews and other minority groups was perhaps the ultimate war on human rights. More than six million people were murdered by the Nazis. When World War II ended, the rest of the world was shocked to discover the extent of the mass murder that had taken place.

Still, out of this human rights catastrophe, progress emerged. Immediately following World War II, the **United Nations (UN)** was formed in October 1945. This international governing organization was set up to create strong alliances among nations even though the people of these nations may have had different beliefs. These nations hoped to prevent another world war. One of the key ideas behind the United Nations was the promotion of human rights. With the beginning of the United Nations, the human rights movement as we know it today was also born.

The Universal Declaration of Human Rights

The United Nations Charter (the document that declared the beginning of the UN) states that the United Nations is committed to faith in "fundamental human rights, in the dignity and worth of the human person, in the equal rights of men and women and of nations large and small … " But the United Nations did not stop there. Three years after its founding, the United Nations adopted the Universal Declaration of Human Rights. This document spelled out all the ways in which individuals' rights must be protected.

CASE STUDY

Eleanor Roosevelt—human rights campaigner

Eleanor Roosevelt was the widow of the three-term president of the United States, Franklin Delano Roosevelt. She had earned a reputation for fighting for individual liberties during her years as the wife of the president. She was appointed as a delegate to the United Nations in 1945 and became the first chairperson of the UN's Commission on Human Rights. Roosevelt was a staunch fighter for human rights, and she worked closely with nations that shared her beliefs and with those that disregarded human rights. She found ways of influencing world leaders to compromise, and, within just two years, she led the United Nations' effort to pass the Universal Declaration of Human Rights. She later wrote, "We wanted as many nations as possible to accept the fact that men, for one reason or another, were born free and equal in dignity and rights."

■ Eleanor Roosevelt celebrates the adoption of the Universal Declaration of Human Rights.

The UN Declaration of Human Rights includes 30 different sections (called articles). Each article defines a different area of human rights, such as the rights to be free from slavery and free from torture and the right to a fair trial—and more. The United Nations passed the Declaration on December 10, 1948. The document is a long and detailed definition of human rights. With this document, the modern human rights movement was launched. Many of these human rights will be explored in this book.

Three generations of human rights

In 1979, Karel Vašák of the International Institute of Human Rights created a way of breaking down human rights into categories that are easy to understand. His Three Generations of Human Rights creates three stages of human rights, based on when they were developed in history.

FIRST GENERATION
Civil and political rights
- right to freedom of speech
- right to a fair trial
- right to freedom of religion
- right to vote
- right to freedom from torture

17th and 18th century

These rights are the same as those that the American and French revolutions were fought for in the 1700s. They are also linked to the thinking of the philosophers in the period called the Enlightenment, in the 1600s to 1700s, which celebrated science and reason.

SECOND GENERATION
Economic, social, cultural rights
- right to employment
- right to education
- right to housing
- right to healthcare
- right to social security and unemployment benefits

19th century

These are rights that people began developing in the 1800s. During the Industrial Revolution, which began in the 1880s, new ideas emerged about privileges such as fair employment and workers' rights.

THIRD GENERATION
Solidarity (group) rights
- right to self-determination
- right to economic development
- right to healthy environment
- right to natural resources
- right to participate in cultural heritage

20th century

These rights began developing in the last half of the 20th century. As nations attempted to overcome poverty, environmental threats, and attacks on ethnic groups, people began to understand that groups of people should have rights that provide for these protections.

THE RIGHT TO LIFE

Article 3 of the UN Declaration of Human Rights establishes that "Everyone has the right to life, liberty and security of person." As we have seen, the 20th century was blackened by the Holocaust, one of the largest slaughters of humanity in history. The United Nations labeled the Holocaust as a **genocide**: the killing of a large portion of an ethnic or religious group with the intent of completely eliminating that group from society.

Unfortunately, the Holocaust was not the only genocide to have taken place in recent times. Murder violates the most basic human right (to life), and murder on a large scale violates the right to life for large populations. Leaders and governments must protect and help their people. Yet, in recent times, we have witnessed leaders deny the right to life for large numbers of their own citizens.

Prisoners of a Nazi concentration camp during the Holocaust.

Hitler and Nazi Germany

In the early 1930s, Adolf Hitler and his political party, the Nazis, took power in Germany by declaring that Germany must be rid of all people who were not "pure" Germans. Once they gained power, they not only invaded other countries in Europe to start World War II, they also waged war in their own country against minorities and any group who was seen as foreign or unfit: Jews, gypsies, homosexuals, those with mental or physical disabilities, and others. The Jews, in particular, were a main target of the Nazis.

The Nazis first abused the rights of these innocent people by passing laws that limited how and where they could live. Later, they moved them out of their homes and into concentration camps. These were huge prisons where many people were tortured and died. The final step was murder on a large scale. Beginning in the early 1940s, the Nazis built death camps, which were factories for murder. The Nazis would transport people into death camps on trains and then kill them in gas chambers. Many others were gunned down in the streets, or pulled out of their homes and taken to remote areas and **executed**. During Hitler's rule, from 1933 to 1945, the Nazis caused the deaths of 17 million people across Europe. Around six million were Jews.

Joseph Stalin

Even before Hitler rose to power, Europe had already suffered under another leader who exercised brutal force against his people. Joseph Stalin led the Soviet Union from the mid-1920s until 1953. Under Stalin, the Soviet Union was a **communist** state, in which the individual's role was to serve the common good. In this system, many key human rights were denied; under Stalin, the right to life was denied to millions.

From 1932 to 1933, a vast famine (starvation) gripped parts of the Soviet Union. Stalin believed that people in the Ukraine region were going to revolt and seek independence. To put down the revolution, he ordered that the Ukrainians receive less grain and other crops than the rest of the Soviet citizens. Millions of Ukrainians died as a result. Many other people died under Stalin's rule. During a period known as the Great **Purge** (1936–1938), the Soviet government arrested more than 1.5 million people who were suspected of working against Stalin. At least 600,000 of these people were killed, and many others were sent to gulags (prison camps in remote locations).

■ In 2009, a ceremony was held in Lviv, Ukraine, to commemorate the victims of the famine of 1932–1933.

Mao Zedong

China was another massive communist country that existed under the thumb of an all-controlling leader, Mao Zedong. Mao took control of China in 1943 and led the country through the Chinese Civil War and the establishment of the People's Republic of China. Throughout his reign over China, political **dissidents**, or people who object to the government, were dealt with harshly. China's Cultural Revolution of 1966 to 1976 was a mass purge of people who challenged Mao's authority. During this period, people who disagreed with communism and the Chinese government were moved to prisons, tortured, and murdered.

Pol Pot

In nearby Cambodia, Pol Pot ruled from 1963 to 1981. He led a disastrous attempt to force millions of city-dwelling Cambodians to become farm workers. Families were moved at gunpoint to "reeducation" camps, to be trained as proper communists and farmers. Many were tortured and murdered in the process.

Pol Pot also dealt harshly with minorities such as Muslims and other religious groups. Countless Cambodian victims of Pol Pot met their tragic deaths in "killing fields," which were vast fields outside of cities where people were murdered. Pol Pot is said to have murdered about two million people.

WHAT DO YOU THINK?

In 2006, Cambodia began trials to punish officials who carried out the murder of Cambodian citizens during Pol Pot's reign. When a dictator leads his nation in mass murder, the dictator himself may not commit a single murder. This work is left to lower-ranking leaders, members of the **militia** (armed civilians), and even ordinary citizens. In a crime such as genocide, millions of people might have become murderers.

Who should be punished for violating a population's right to life? Should only the leaders be put on trial, or should courts try to punish every person who took part in the murders?

Nicholae Ceausescu

Another dictator who rose to power in the last half of the 20th century was Nicholae Ceausescu of Romania. From 1965 to 1989, Ceausescu suppressed the rights of his people and gradually built a "cult of personality" in which his followers worshipped him like a hero. Ceausescu did not kill citizens on as large a scale as Hitler, Stalin, or Mao, but he did control Romanians' lives in repressive ways. When the Romanian economy struggled in the early 1980s, Ceausescu left thousands without support, food, electricity, or medical care, all of which are human rights. According to Article 25 of the UN Declaration of Human Rights, everyone has the right to a standard of living, which includes adequate food and proper housing and medical care. While his citizens lived in terrible conditions, Ceausescu and his family lived a lavish, rich lifestyle. One report states that he owned 22,000 suits.

Ceausescu was eventually overthrown in December 1989. His military had opened fire on a demonstrating crowd, killing 4,000 people. An even greater crowd of 100,000 gathered a week later and shouted Ceausescu down when he attempted to speak to them. He and his wife then fled the country, but they were captured, put on trial, and shot by a firing squad.

■ This photo shows Romanian dictator Nicholae Ceausescu making a speech, days before he was overthrown.

CASE STUDY

Reproductive rights

In the 1960s, Nicholae Ceausescu wanted to increase the population of Romania, so he banned abortions and birth control. In effect, he forced women to have more babies. He said, "Anyone who avoids having children is a deserter who abandons the laws of national continuity." In China, an opposite concern caused a different law to be put in place. In 1979, the Chinese government, worried about overpopulation, made it illegal for families to have more than one child.

In the UN Declaration of Human Rights, Article 16 includes protections of the family against a government. It says, "The family is the natural and fundamental group unit of society and is entitled to protection by society and the State." This rule does not necessarily protect people against the types of rules that Romania, China, and other countries have imposed. In 1968, the United Nations held an International Conference on Human Rights in Tehran, Iran, at which the organization looked back at the Declaration of Human Rights. At the Tehran conference, additional guidelines were written that expanded on some of the ideas in the original declaration. One area that was expanded includes family planning. The conference decided, "Parents have a basic human right to determine freely and responsibly the number and spacing of their children." This means that a government should not be able to force a family to have a certain number of children.

Saddam Hussein

The late 20th century saw dictators rise up in several Arab countries. Saddam Hussein became president of Iraq in 1979 and controlled the country for more than two decades. Among many human rights violations committed by Saddam was his treatment of the Kurdish people in the late 1980s. Living mainly in northern Iraq, the Kurds sought independence, and Saddam struck them down by attacking them not only with armed forces, but with poisonous gas, killing at least 5,000 people in 1988. This was just one attack in Saddam's attempt to exterminate the Iraqi Kurds. In all, more than 180,000 Kurds lost their lives.

"Before dawn, as people were getting dressed and ready to go to work, all the soldiers charged through the camp ... They took the preacher who went to the mosque to call for prayers. They were breaking down doors and entering the houses searching for our men."

A Kurdish woman who survived describes an attack by Iraqi forces on her village

Ayatollah Khomeini

In 1979, the same year that Saddam Hussein took power in Iraq, a revolt placed the religious leader Ayatollah Khomeini in control in neighboring Iran. He quickly transformed Iran into a country ruled by Islamic law. In such a culture, there are strict rules for how people may behave. For instance, strict Muslims believe in treating men and women differently in society. Under Islamic law in Iran, Khomeini passed laws forcing women to dress a certain way, to not hold certain jobs (he removed all women judges), and to prevent them from participating in activities with men, such as swimming.

THE HUNT FOR WMDs

Saddam Hussein's use of chemical weapons against his own people helped to fuel suspicion around the world that Iraq was again developing "weapons of mass destruction": chemical or nuclear weapons that could kill large numbers of people. In 2003, Western allies, including the United Kingdom and the United States, invaded Iraq and removed Saddam and his government from power. Saddam was eventually tried by an Iraqi court and executed in 2006.

However, when the invading forces found no evidence of Saddam's weapons of mass destruction, critics claimed that the United Kingdom and the United States had invented the excuse for the invasion. The British prime minister, Tony Blair, and the president of the United States, George W. Bush, defended their actions, saying that they had succeeded in liberating Iraq from a cruel dictator.

Was it wrong for Prime Minister Blair and President Bush to use weapons of mass destruction as the reason for the invasion?

■ A statue of Saddam Hussein is toppled in 2003 after he is removed from power.

Like other all-powerful leaders, Khomeini did not allow **dissent**. People who had worked for the former government were imprisoned and tortured. Some were even killed. In 1988, Khomeini launched a religious law called a fatwa against all those who were perceived as enemies. Within a year, as many as 30,000 political enemies were killed under the fatwa, including the spouses and children of those enemies.

FREEDOM FROM RELIGION?

Article 18 of the Universal Declaration of Human Rights declares that everyone has the right to freedom of religion. Clearly, this means that countries such as Iran, which are controlled by strict Islamic law, are prone to violate the human rights of their citizens. However, even in democracies, tensions exist between the force of religious belief and human rights. For instance, in the United States, homosexuals have fought for certain rights for a long time. The rights have been denied partly due to a strong belief by Christians in government that homosexuality is wrong. Religious beliefs also drive many people to support a ban on abortion.

Should religious beliefs be considered when creating any laws that govern how people live their lives?

The Taliban

As shown by the actions of Ayatollah Khomeini and other dictators, societies ruled by strict religious beliefs often infringe on human rights. In the mid-1990s, Afghanistan fell under the rule of the Taliban, a militia group with extreme views about the teachings of Islam. They used terror to rise to power beginning in 1994, before they finally seized control of Afghanistan's government in 1996. They ruled for five years in which the Afghan people lived in fear of violence and death. The Taliban went on a killing spree as they attempted to eliminate ethnic groups who might oppose them. Hundreds of Pashtuns, Hazaras, and other groups of Afghans were killed as armed militia groups invaded their villages. Men, women, and children were shot in the street. A United Nations report published in 2001 included witness accounts of people lined up and shot by firing squads with their hands tied behind their backs. All of the attacks were highly organized and were linked to the head of the Taliban, Mohammed Omar.

DIFFICULT QUESTIONS

In 2001, the Taliban ruler Mullah Mohammed Omar stated that anyone in Afghanistan who converts from Islam to another religion would be punished with the death penalty. Even though the Taliban is no longer in power, the threat of death still exists for Afghan Muslims who leave the Islamic religion. In some countries, such as the United States, the death penalty can be imposed on criminals who are convicted of extremely serious murders. In other countries, drug trafficking is punishable by death. In 2008, the ten countries that carried out the most executions were: China, Iran, Saudi Arabia, the United States, Pakistan, Iraq, Vietnam, Afghanistan, North Korea, and Japan.

Human rights **advocates** argue that the death penalty is an improper way of punishing any criminal, no matter what the crime. Most nations' governments agree. The death penalty has been outlawed in every country in Western Europe, among other places.

Do you think it is right to kill a criminal for certain crimes? If so, which crimes should be punishable by death?

In Iran and other countries, the government uses execution to punish criminals.

PRISONERS' RIGHTS

When governments torture or murder their own citizens, it is difficult to deny that a blatant human rights crime has been committed. However, what are the rights of citizens who themselves have committed crimes? Does someone who has infringed on others' human rights have human rights? Human rights advocates work to ensure that prisoners' rights are protected in several areas.

Conditions of confinement

Some law-abiding citizens may feel that prisons should not be comfortable places to live. But human rights advocates argue that prisoners still deserve clean living quarters that are not overcrowded. Prison systems cope with prison overcrowding, especially when government budgets are tight and the expense of building new prisons is high. Prisoners are also sometimes denied their right to proper medical care, their right to free expression (to say or write what they wish), their right to freedom of religion, and other rights.

Treatment by authorities

One of the most difficult issues for both prisoners and prison authorities is the way in which prisoners are treated. In a confined space filled with violent criminals, it can be difficult to maintain discipline. Prison officers sometimes have to use force to maintain order and to protect prisoners and other staff. However, in some countries, prison officers beat or torture prisoners for punishment. Prisoners might be beaten if authorities are trying to force them to provide information or to confess to a crime.

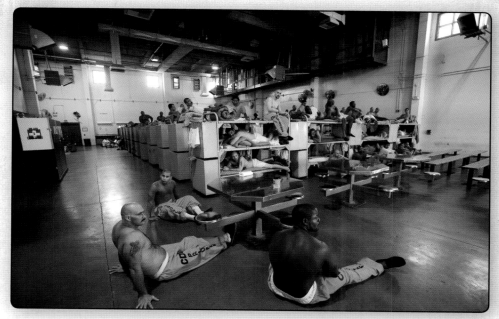

■ In overcrowded prisons, the prisoners lack privacy and healthy living conditions. Here the prisoners sleep in cramped bunkbeds.

Due process

Article 10 of the UN Declaration of Human Rights states that everyone is entitled to a fair and public trial. People who are arrested and sent to prison must be provided with a lawyer and given a fair trial. This is called due process, referring to the appropriate procedure that the legal system must follow. But some people are held in prison without due process. They may be charged with crimes but never brought to trial. Immigrants to a country who may not have the same status as citizens of that country are sometimes at risk of being denied due process. And individuals who are suspected of war crimes or terrorism have also been held without due process.

Political prisoners

There are many independent organizations that monitor human rights abuses around the world. One of the most prominent groups is **Amnesty** International. It was founded in 1961 by a British lawyer named Peter Benenson. He had heard about two students in Portugal who had been held in prison for seven years after being arrested but not tried. In direct response to a case of prisoners' rights, an important, worldwide organization began.

The word *amnesty* refers to a person being forgiven for a crime or other offense. Benenson formed Amnesty International to be a group that would be advocates for prisoners whose rights were being denied by the governments holding them without due process, or for prisoners who were being mistreated. In the early 1960s, Amnesty International started using the term *prisoners of conscience* to describe people who were sent to prison for expressing ideas about their beliefs, lifestyle, race, or religion in a nonviolent way. These prisoners have not committed any acts of violence.

Prisoners may be convicted on invented charges in which a government exaggerates the case against them or hands down a sentence that is much harsher than the crime warrants. They are imprisoned because they protested against the government. Today such people are also called political prisoners.

Monitoring human rights abuses

Amnesty International is one of many organizations that monitors human rights abuses around the world. The United Nations, **Human Rights Watch**, and Amnesty International have established a network of people such as lawyers, religious leaders, teachers, and healthcare workers who live in regions all over the world. These people are trained to watch for signs that local tensions are threatening human rights. Monitors notify the larger organizations, which react in a number of ways.

The United Nations can put pressure on nations to stop human rights abuses. Other organizations use the media to publicize situations so that the public and world leaders know what is happening. These organizations can place pressure on human rights abusers through a number of measures. They can name specific people (from terrorist leaders to military leaders to the rulers of nations) whom they believe are responsible for abuses. They sometimes launch letter-writing campaigns in which they instruct people around the world to send letters to their own government leaders to demand action against the abuses. And they contact large corporations doing business in the countries where the abuse takes place and demand that these companies threaten to stop doing business there. This places an economic pressure on the nation where the crimes are taking place.

■ In 2011, Aung San Suu Kyi presented two of the prestigious BBC Reith Lectures. Her lectures were secretly filmed in Burma and smuggled out to be broadcast from London.

House arrest

When a criminal is sentenced to house arrest, it usually means that the crime committed was so minor that the person does not need to serve a punishment in prison. However, the term has taken on a new meaning, as governments sometimes place political dissidents under house arrest. Human rights groups believe this is a way that some governments repress individuals without going so far as to torture or imprison them. Instead, they force the person to stay in their home, unable to travel and often unable to communicate with the outside world. Some house arrests have lasted for years.

In Burma in 1990, the politician Aung San Suu Kyi campaigned as a candidate for prime minister against the military party that had recently overtaken the country. Suu Kyi won the election, but the militia refused to accept the election results and placed her under house arrest. She was put under house arrest several different times for a total of more than 15 years, from 1990 until her release on November 13, 2010. She was awarded the Nobel Peace Prize in 1991 for her work, but, as she was under house arrest, she could not travel to Sweden to attend the ceremony. Her sons accepted the award for her.

Prisoners of war

One of the most difficult prisoners' rights issues is that of prisoners of war, soldiers who are captured and held as prisoners by an enemy army. For much of the 20th century, several international agreements were in place regarding how captured soldiers were to be treated by their captors. The Geneva Convention is a set of rules written in 1929 and revised in 1949. Most nations recognize the convention. It states that prisoners of war must not be tortured and that the prisoners are not required to give any information except to identify themselves. In times of war, however, many governments have not followed the Geneva Convention. In some wars, prisoners have been tortured and killed.

Detention centers

The United States set up a detention center (prison) at its naval base at Guantánamo Bay, Cuba. In 2002, it began holding prisoners who were suspected of being terrorists or having ties to terrorists. In 2004, the Americans set up another such prison at Abu Ghraib, Iraq.

President Bush described the men held in these prisons not as prisoners of war, but as unlawful combatants. Because they were not prisoners of war, the president claimed that the Geneva Convention protections did not apply to them.

These blindfolded prisoners are being taken for questioning. Abuses and torture may take place in many detention centers.

In these detention centers, prisoners were tortured, sexually abused, drugged, and harmed by other violent acts. In some cases, the guards used violent methods to force the prisoners to provide information about terrorist activities. In other cases, it has been proved that prisoners were tortured for no apparent reason. At Guantánamo, some prisoners were subjected to **waterboarding**, a brutal treatment that is intended to weaken a prisoner to the point where he will reveal any information. The prisoner is tied down to a board, tipped so his feet are in the air, and water is poured over his head. The prisoner has the sensation of drowning and suffers from gagging and panic.

The United States has been strongly criticized by its enemies, its **allies**, and its own citizens for the actions at Guantánamo and Abu Ghraib. Critics claim that by treating prisoners in this way, the government is denying these prisoners their human rights.

CASE STUDY

"War on terror"

On September 11, 2001, many nations' ideas about war changed. On that day, teams of men working with the al-Qaeda terrorist group boarded several commercial airplanes as ordinary passengers. They took control of the planes and crashed them into key buildings in the United States. More than 2,700 people died in the attacks. While this was not the first terrorist attack against American civilians, it was the largest scale attack on U.S. soil.

The president of the United States, George W. Bush, immediately declared a "war on terror." He told the world that this would be an unusual war. The United States was not at war with a single country. Instead, its enemy was to some extent unknown—terrorists hiding within various foreign nations. The U.S. military attacked several suspected terrorist cells, or teams, and also set up an extensive **surveillance** network in an attempt to find terrorists and stop them before they committed any further acts.

CHILDREN'S RIGHTS

The Declaration of the Rights of the Child was written in 1923. It was later accepted by international organizations, including the United Nations, in 1959. This document outlines many rights for children, such as follows: children should be given special care because they are not able to care for themselves; children must be given proper medical care, shelter, and education; in times of crisis, children must be given protection and care before adults.

Children in the workplace

In past societies, children led different lives from children today. Before the 1800s, for example, there were no school systems or other settings to educate, entertain, and nurture children as they grew up. In the past, many children worked. For instance, children who grew up on farms would usually do farm work, some of which was difficult and possibly dangerous.

The boundaries separating children from manual labor began to arise during the Industrial Revolution, which began in the 1800s. As more work was being done in factories with huge machines, it gradually became clear to child advocates and governments that children needed protection. Some of this work was quite dangerous and not appropriate for children. Some factories were dirty or gave off fumes that harmed children more than adults. And the poorer the child, the more pressure he or she was under to make money. Some children worked as many as 16 hours per day. Throughout the 1800s and into the 1900s, governments passed laws to protect children from such dangers.

WHAT DO YOU THINK?

What is the difference between a child working on a family farm and a child working in a factory? Does a family have the right to put its children to work on its own farm if the same child is not allowed to work in a factory or other place of business?

■ A nine-year-old boy works in unsafe conditions in a balloon factory in Bangladesh.

Child labor today

The 1959 United Nations document on children's rights stated that children must not be put to work before an appropriate age, and many nations have firm laws in place to protect children from unfair or dangerous workplaces. Even so, **UNICEF** (the United Nations Children's Fund) estimates that about 158 million children between the ages of 5 and 14 are laborers. That is equivalent to 1 out of every 6 children in the world. Many working children are exposed to dangers to their health, such as Alone Banda, who crushed boulders into gravel. In the remote coal-mining towns in Kyrgyzstan, children often work in the coal mines. This is dangerous because children who inhale toxic substances in coal mines can suffer lung damage for life.

It is not only children in **developing countries** who are at risk. In 2008, the U.S. government shut down a meat-packing factory in Iowa because it was found that children were working long hours and doing dangerous work with sharp knives and saws.

Placing pressure on companies

Consumers around the world have become outraged to hear stories of children working long hours in dangerous factories for very little pay. In recent years, they have found ways to stop these practices. For instance, it was discovered that many large companies used child labor in foreign countries or otherwise abused their adult workers' rights. Consumers staged several successful **boycotts** against these companies. This means they protested by refusing to buy their products. Other companies have been forced to reverse their unfair labor practices after being exposed in the news media.

In the 1990s, consumers put pressure on the Nike company to stop using factories in Cambodia to make footballs because the factories employed children in unsafe conditions. In 2007, the multinational clothing company Gap was proven to be using 10- to 13-year-old children to stitch clothing in factories in India. The company said it had not realized the factories were using child labor, and they stopped using those factories.

Child warriors

When a nation goes to war, it struggles with the idea that its young men and women will suffer. In most countries, the youngest soldiers must be at least 18 years old by law.

However, throughout history, children of much younger ages have gone to war. In some wars, young boys were used as messengers to carry important information, or girls were used to help provide medical assistance. But children are also used on the front lines of armed conflicts. They even carry and use weapons. In a 2008 report, the Human Rights Watch group found that between 2004 and 2007, nineteen countries used children under 18 years of age to fight in armed conflicts. These countries included Afghanistan, Colombia, India, Iraq, Israel, the Philippines, and Sudan. There were many more instances of children being recruited for use in illegal militias or secret police units that are not part of a country's normal army. Overall, it was estimated that there were tens of thousands of child soldiers in the world in 2007.

WHAT DO YOU THINK?

When large companies choose to stop (or are forced to stop) using child labor, they dismiss the children working in those factories or even shut the factories down and look for labor elsewhere. By solving the problem of children's rights, even more suffering can be created for the workers. They lose their jobs, and they fall deeper into poverty. Children work because they—and their families—need the money. If their jobs disappear, they may be in an even worse situation because they lose what little money they were earning.

Some organizations, such as Fair Trade, run programs to help resolve these issues. Fair Trade works with companies to find ways of saving costs on producing goods and turning those cost savings into investments in the communities where the workers live. For instance, Fair Trade may start education programs to help children in a community.

Do you think it is right or wrong for a company to dismiss child laborers who need the money they are earning, if the company does not provide safe conditions?

■ Support organizations may provide learning materials in places where children would otherwise not be able to go to school.

■ This Liberian soldier is only nine years old.

Brainwashing children to kill

How, exactly, can a young child be turned into a soldier? Quite often, children are brainwashed. They are stolen from their homes and separated from their families. They are trained in a way to make them forget about their former lives and to forget about the sense of right and wrong that they may have developed. They are trained to follow any orders, no matter how cruel, even if that means killing or torturing other human beings.

By 2009, at least 76 countries had signed an agreement on the legal minimum age for joining the military. This age was set at 18 years old. However, a United Nations report published in 2010 estimates that more than 250,000 children around the world are involved with armed groups or armed forces. This may include being forced to work as cooks or porters as well as soldiers. UNICEF works for the release of children who are taken away by fighting forces. It also helps when children are freed from fighting as soldiers for those forces.

CASE STUDY

A child trained to kill

Ishmael Beah grew up in Sierra Leone. When his village was set ablaze by rebel soldiers in 1993, his parents and siblings were murdered, and he was cast out on his own for months. The Sierra Leone army eventually captured him, trained him, brainwashed him, and got him addicted to drugs to gain more control over him. In less than a year, at the age of 13, he had become a murderer. He went out on raids and regularly killed rebel soldiers. He later wrote that after his first killing, "The idea of death didn't cross my mind, and killing had become as easy as drinking water."

Two years later, representatives of UNICEF rescued Ishmael from his army troop. He was taken to a rehabilitation hospital, where he endured a long, difficult process of "relearning boyhood." He had completely forgotten how to behave as a normal boy. Ishmael also had to be cured of his drug addiction. He had nightmares related to memories of his years as a warrior and suffered from not understanding how to relate to people except as a killer. He later said that it was harder to learn how not to be a killer than it was to learn to kill. After rehabilitation, Ishmael moved to the United States and went to college in Ohio. He wrote a book about his childhood called *A Long Way Gone.*

■ Today, Ishmael Beah works with Human Rights Watch and other groups that strive to protect children's rights.

CITIZENS' RIGHTS

Article 21 of the UN Declaration of Human Rights states that all individuals have the right to be a citizen, which means having the freedom to participate in government. One of the main ways that citizens participate in government is to vote in elections. However, voting is not a right that all people enjoy.

Voting rights

As democracy has spread, the right to vote has been a hard-won battle. In most countries of the world, women were not allowed the right to vote until the last century or so. In 1893, the British colony of New Zealand gave women the right to vote, and nearby Australia followed in 1902. By that time, women's suffrage (right to vote) protests were common in many other countries. However, it was not until 1920 that the United States allowed women the right to vote on the same terms as men. By then many other countries had already passed similar laws.

Today, the ability to vote in free and open elections is still a right that many people are denied. Some leaders may hold elections but use force to make sure of a certain outcome. President Robert Mugabe of Zimbabwe has been accused of holding unfair elections ever since he won control of his country in 1987. In 2002, for example, Mugabe's government was accused of allowing its supporters to register to vote for months after the deadline passed. Mugabe was also said to have set up more polling stations (places to vote) available in areas where his supporters lived. And during the election itself, Mugabe's police force drove his opponents away from polling stations using tear gas and batons to beat those people who resisted. There were also reports that the voting results were changed and that votes by opposition supporters were not all counted.

CASE STUDY

An ex-president fights for human rights

To attempt to preserve citizens' voting rights, several international organizations operate as election monitors and observe elections. Jimmy Carter, the former president of the United States, founded the Carter Center in 1982 as an organization that works for human rights around the world. The organization has sent teams of impartial experts to 33 countries and has observed more than 80 elections. Sometimes Carter leads the teams himself. Election monitors do not interfere in elections. They simply observe and write reports on what happens. Monitors can help ensure fair elections because all opposing sides in an election know that any wrongdoing will be made public. South Africa's Archbishop Desmond Tutu said, "When it comes to elections, Carter is the most listened to voice in the world."

The Carter Center is involved in many other activities related to human rights, solving health issues in nations stricken by poverty, and negotiating peaceful solutions to conflicts. Carter has written, "We can choose to alleviate suffering. We can choose to work together for peace. We can make these changes—and we must."

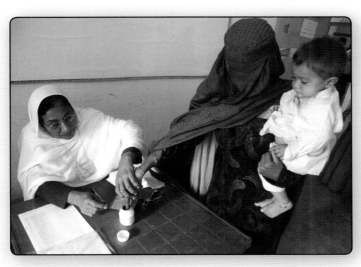

■ A woman in Afghanistan votes in a 2010 election.

Rights affect lives

While voting rights are crucial in maintaining a free society, there are other human rights that can have an even greater impact on people's everyday lives. The following are just a few important citizens' rights that are named in the UN's Declaration of Human Rights.

- *The right to free access to government services and protections* – This right is a guarantee that governments will treat all citizens equally. If a government provides free healthcare to some of its citizens, it cannot deny healthcare to others. Police forces and armies must protect all groups of citizens equally and not leave some groups in danger.

- *The right to free movement* – The right to free movement means that people should be able to come and go as they wish. They should be able to travel outside their home country, and they should be able to return home as well. Some countries stop the movement of dissidents so that these people will not be able to work against the government. Other countries force people to live in certain areas of the country. This kind of restriction does not allow them to choose the best places to get good homes, schools, and healthcare.

- *The right to have a nationality* – Each individual's nationality is that of the country where he or she is a citizen. A person's nationality is important to have a sense of identity, but even more important are the legal protections and entitlements that come with nationality. In fair and free nations, citizens are protected by their governments. If people are not allowed to have a nationality and become citizens, they are not able to benefit from these privileges. Today, the largest number of people who lack a nationality are about ten million Palestinian Arabs who live outside the Palestinian homeland of Israel and the occupied territories.

When a government denies the human rights of its citizens, the citizens grow angry, and they may try to revolt and remove those in charge. This occurred in the "Arab Spring" of 2011. Beginning in late December 2010 and continuing for several months, people in Tunisia, Egypt, Libya, Syria, and other Arabic-speaking countries launched mass protests against their governments. In Libya, all-out civil war broke out between the government and the people. In Egypt, the people's protests were heard and a change of power took place. Egypt's president Hosni Mubarak was forced out of office after having controlled the country since 1981.

WHAT DO YOU THINK?

The Palestinians are Arabic-speaking people whose roots lie in Palestine, which is today called Israel. For years, the Palestinians and the Jewish state of Israel have been in conflict over which group owns the rights to the land. Some Palestinians live in Israel, but nearly four million Palestinians live in two small areas: the West Bank and the Gaza Strip. Israel controls the borders to these areas and controls who may come and go across the borders into Israel. Part of Israel's stated purpose is to keep terrorists out of Israel. Palestinians complain that they are barred from crossing the border to jobs, to hospitals, or to visit family. Border control is just one of the many heated issues that divide Israelis and Palestinians.

When a border exists between two countries, which country should have control over it?

Mediterranean Sea

SYRIA

ISRAEL

West Bank

Jerusalem
Gaza Strip

Dead
Sea

EGYPT

JORDAN

These Palestinian women are lining up at a checkpoint in the West Bank to cross into Israel to attend a mosque in Jerusalem.

CASE STUDY

South Africa's human rights revolution

South Africa was once a British colony. Under British rule, the native black people who lived there were given very few rights. They could not move freely from one district to another; they could not hold certain jobs; they could not receive the same level of services such as medical care and education as white people. Black South Africans were an oppressed people, despite the fact that they had lived in South Africa much longer than the white Europeans who ruled them. South Africa gained its independence from the United Kingdom in 1934, but oppression of the blacks continued.

Apartheid

In 1948, the white-led South African government officially adopted a policy called **apartheid**. Under apartheid, the South African government enacted many laws that officially separated white people from black Africans and other racial groups. Apartheid laws forced the different races to live in separate regions, banned marriages between the races, and created separate services such as schools and hospitals, and even park benches. All of the laws were intended to provide whites with the greater advantages in society and to keep blacks at a disadvantage, further and further out of contact with whites.

Black South Africans attempted to fight back, although it was difficult and dangerous to do so. An organization called the African National Congress (ANC) was formed in 1912 to fight for South African's equal rights.

A leader emerges

In the 1940s, a leader emerged in the ANC who would eventually topple apartheid decades later. Nelson Mandela was a young lawyer who was committed to fighting for his people's rights. He organized and inspired the ANC to use nonviolent ways of protesting, such as strikes and boycotts. In 1952, the government issued a "ban" on Mandela, restricting his travel and not allowing him to meet with more than three people at a time. Mandela continued to do his anti-apartheid work, and after being arrested and found not guilty in a trial, Mandela went underground (working in secret) to continue plotting and working against the government. He worked in disguises so that he could escape the notice of police and be able to continue organizing the ANC.

The Sharpeville Massacre

On March 21, 1960, a group of protesters was demonstrating in the township of Sharpeville. Reports disagree on whether the protests were completely peaceful. However, one fact is certain. The protesters far outnumbered the South African police who were present. At a certain point in the day, the police opened fire on the crowd, killing 69 black people. The Sharpeville Massacre was a turning point for Mandela and other ANC leaders. They decided that they must match violence with violence, and the ANC began engaging in armed combat with the authorities.

■ Bodies of victims of the 1960 Sharpeville massacre lie on the ground.

Political prisoner

In 1962, the police finally arrested Nelson Mandela. He was put on trial and was convicted by an all-white jury. He was sentenced to five years in prison, but a later trial for additional crimes resulted in a life sentence. In 1964, Mandela and other ANC activists were sent to prison. However, Mandela not only survived prison but continued his anti-apartheid work as much as he could. He read, he wrote, he had secret communications with other prisoners and ANC organizers on the outside, and he educated many other black prisoners on the need to fight apartheid.

After 20 years in prison, the work of Mandela and his allies was having an effect. The message had spread across the globe. By the mid-1980s, intense pressure was being placed on the South African government to reform the apartheid laws. Beginning in 1985, leaders of the government started talking to Mandela, who was still a prisoner, about ways of reaching a compromise. The breakthrough came in 1989, when South African President P. W. Botha suffered a stroke and was replaced by Frederik Willem de Klerk, who recognized the need for an end to the conflict.

Conquering hero

On February 11, 1990, Nelson Mandela walked out of prison as a free man. At the same time, President de Klerk ended all bans on the ANC. In South Africa and around the world, human rights activitists and informed world citizens rejoiced as Mandela's release was shown on live television. Mandela had accomplished the incredible feat of bringing a brutal government to its knees.

Over the next four years, Mandela led negotiations with de Klerk and the South African government on how to end apartheid. The apartheid era finally ended in 1994 when Mandela was elected president of South Africa. He then proceeded to dismantle the laws of apartheid and set South Africa on a path to equal rights.

Truth and reconciliation

With victory in hand, Nelson Mandela still faced the difficult task of moving South Africa forward. Following such a long, bitter, and violent struggle, the entire society needed a way of recognizing the events of the conflict and finding ways for people to live in peace. This process is reconciliation, and it can be fraught with difficulties.

Mandela's new government established a Truth and Reconciliation Commission soon after apartheid ended. The commission was built to allow people to come forward and tell the truth about what happened during apartheid. This process of bearing witness is necessary to provide victims the opportunity to hear their stories told in public, so they know their struggles will not be forgotten by history.

The commission was not set up to prosecute criminals as most war-crimes trials do. It was meant more as a way for all sides of the conflict to reveal the truth of apartheid. In its final report, the commission laid blame with both the government and with anti-apartheid activists for the violence they employed. The commission granted amnesty to the perpetrators of human rights crimes. Although the process provided comfort and closure for some people, many black Africans felt that justice and punishment would have been a better conclusion to their difficult struggle.

GENDER, RACE, AND CULTURAL RIGHTS

In many countries where there is relative peace and a strong democratic government rules, there are still human rights issues to address. Sometimes, human rights crimes occur behind a wall of secrecy and only come out into the open years later. At other times, human rights crimes might concern issues that are not matters of life and death but are very important, nonetheless. The United Nations (UN) Declaration of Human Rights declares in Article 1: "All humans are born free and equal." All humans include ourselves, our fellow citizens, and our neighbors. Sometimes we are shocked to find that human rights violations occur in our own country.

Indigenous peoples' rights

In 2007, the United Nations adopted the Declaration of Rights of Indigenous Peoples. Indigenous peoples are groups who have a historical link to a land. They are people and nations who lived in a place before other explorers, settlers, or conquerors arrived and set up their own communities. For centuries, the human rights of indigenous peoples have been cast aside as newcomers set up new societies. In the UN's original Declaration of Human Rights, indigenous peoples were not named specifically. However, after years of struggle, their rights were finally recognized in 2007.

One of the most tragic recent examples of indigenous rights abuses concerned the Australian Aboriginals and Torres Strait Islanders. Australian Aboriginals are indigenous people who speak a wide variety of languages, and who lived on the continent of Australia for thousands of years before British colonists arrived in the late 1700s. Torres Strait Islanders trace their roots to civilizations on a group of 274 islands between Australia and New Zealand. Together, the two groups make up about 450,000 of Australia's 21.8 million people. Throughout the years, the indigenous people suffered as they were mistreated, denied rights, and forced off their native lands.

From 1910 to 1970, the Australian government forcibly removed babies and older children from their parents' care and moved these children to be raised in separate institutions. The government's intention was to reduce the size and strength of the Aboriginal population by continually weeding out its youngest children. The victims of this policy came to be known as the Stolen Generations.

In the 1960s, the Australian government began the attempt to restore the rights of its indigenous peoples. In 2000, Prime Minister John Howard issued a sweeping apology to the Aboriginal people for years of abuse, and the government passed a Motion of Reconciliation. In 2008, Australia went further in repairing the past. Prime Minister Kevin Rudd again apologized openly and publicly and at great length for the Stolen Generations.

■ This Aboriginal father and his children are in Arnhem Land, a region of Australia that has been occupied by indigenous people for tens of thousands of years.

Other nations have come to terms with their own difficult relations with indigenous peoples. In the United States, centuries of struggle and outright war with the many different American Indian tribes and nations has gradually moved toward peace in the last half-century. In 1975, the U.S. government passed the Indian Self-Determination and Education Assistance Act. This law shifted the relationship between American Indians and the government. American Indian nations were encouraged to establish themselves as autonomous (self-governing) communities, with their own businesses and industries that they could profit from. The right to self-determination (having a nationality) is provided for in Article 15 of the UN Declaration of Human Rights.

Women's rights

When the Taliban took power in Afghanistan, they stated that they wished to bring order to Afghanistan by creating a strict Islamic society. Under Taliban rule, women were treated especially poorly, forced to wear **burqas** in public to cover their faces, forced out of school, and forced out of jobs. Women were punished for breaking rules, with vicious beatings in public.

To people living in democratic societies, such treatment may sound strange. Yet, it was less than a century ago when women in just about every nation of the world were denied key human rights. One of the first major victories for women's rights was the right to vote in elections (see page 36). In the 1960s and 1970s, women began gaining many more rights that had traditionally been denied to them. In 1975, the British government passed several laws that made it possible for women to be hired for any job and to earn equal pay for those jobs. Other countries in Europe soon passed similar laws that banned discrimination based on gender.

Today, women in most Western societies are just as likely to hold jobs as doctors, lawyers, business executives, and in government as men are. One of the last roles in which women do not have equal footing with men is in the military. While many Western nations have integrated women into their armed services, very few allow women to take part in active combat. Countries that do allow women an active combat role include Canada, France, Germany, and Israel.

■ The Taliban forced the women of Afghanistan to wear burqas that completely cover them.

Despite this progress, there are places where women still suffer violations of their human rights. In some cultures, a woman is required to stay at home and not enter the working world. Or, in societies where women do work, they may not be treated fairly if they become pregnant.

There are much harsher ways in which women are still mistreated. In several African countries, for instance, women are not allowed to own property. In some countries, there are no laws to protect women from **domestic violence**. And, most tragically, in places where war breaks out, women have sometimes been treated with vicious cruelty. When civilian populations come under attack, armies often attempt to humiliate and devastate the population. They often resort to raping (sexually attacking) women, in addition to other methods of torture and murder.

THE MODERN SLAVE TRADE

Slavery is one of the most extreme human rights violations. There is no self-determination for a slave. There is no citizenship for a slave. There is certainly no freedom for a slave. Some people may believe that slavery was abolished long ago, but, in our present society, there are still people who are captured and sold into slavery. Today's slave owners typically look for people who can work as laborers or as prostitutes (those who sell themselves for sex).

In Sudan, India, Haiti, Pakistan, and other countries, people who are desperately poor will do almost anything to work and earn a living. This practice also occurs with illegal immigrants in the United States.

Sometimes, people owe money to the employer, and their debt keeps them in slavery. In other cases, people are simply kidnapped and forced into slavery at gunpoint. These slaves are then put to work in factories or forced to do dangerous, difficult work such as mining or road building. The conditions can be terrible, and, if a worker falls ill or is injured, the owner is unlikely to provide any medical care.

Another way slaves are used is for prostitution. Girls and young women are kidnapped, often forced into drug addiction, and then forced to earn money for their owners as prostitutes.

Slaves are bought and sold surprisingly cheaply. According to the organization Free the Slaves, it costs an average of $82 to buy a slave today. This is because slave traders are able to capture many slaves very easily.

Gay rights

While the 20th century saw many Western nations embrace equal rights movements supporting women and racial minorities, the early 2000s has seen another group make strides in its pursuit of equality. Gays and lesbians have been seeking the rights to live their lives as equal members of society for many years. Now governments are beginning to recognize those rights.

As recently as the 1970s, doctors treated homosexuality as a mental disorder, an illness of the mind. In 1967, the British government ruled that sex between gay men was no longer a criminal act, and, in the United States, the same decision was reached by state governments through the 1970s and '80s. In recent years, the gay rights movement has turned its focus to seeking protection from discrimination.

The right to serve in the military is not a right that has been outlined in human rights documents. However, gay rights advocates claim that every citizen should have the right to participate in society equally and without discrimination, and this means they should be able to serve in the military. However, for years, gays have been kept out of the military in many societies. In 1993, President Bill Clinton introduced the "Don't Ask, Don't Tell" policy in the U.S. military. This controversial law allowed gays and lesbians to serve in the military, but it did not allow army officials to ask applicants about their sexual orientation. In 1999, the British military began allowing gays and lesbians to join without any restrictions. It also banned discrimination against gays in the military.

Today, gay rights advocates are fighting for the right to have gay marriages recognized by governments. In Canada, Sweden, Norway, the Netherlands, Belgium, Spain, Iceland, South Africa, Argentina, and in several states in the United States, gays and lesbians have the right to legal marriage. Civil partnerships in the United Kingdom give full legal rights to gays and lesbians in registered relationships. In many other places, gays and lesbians have limited rights to civil ceremonies.

Religious rights

A passionately divisive area of human rights is the freedom of religious expression. Religion has inspired some of the greatest acts of kindness, charity, art, and beauty in human history. Religion has also been used to justify some of the most brutal wars and some of the most repressive governments.

According to a 2009 study, countries such as Canada, Brazil, and the United Kingdom are among countries with the fewest examples of violence or restrictions of human rights due to religion. Brazil, for example, has developed a reputation as one of the most tolerant countries in the world. Its constitution guarantees that all people can practice any religion, and its population is a true melting pot of ethnic and religious groups.

On the other hand, nations such as North Korea, Iran, China, Egypt, and Saudi Arabia are among the most intolerant toward religious freedoms. In Saudi Arabia, for example, the government does not recognize that freedom of religion is a right. It is a society ruled strictly by the laws of Islam, and the punishments for breaking these laws are severe. In Saudi Arabia, every citizen must be a Muslim, and it is even illegal to display symbols of other religions, such as a Christian crucifix or a Jewish star of David.

CASE STUDY

Falun Gong challenges China

The government of China is known for controlling the rights of its citizens in many ways. However, Chinese people are allowed a certain amount of religious freedom. The majority of Chinese people follow Buddhism, Taoism, or one of the Chinese folk religions. In 1999, a new spiritual group was created in China, and the government disapproved of it. This has resulted in an ongoing human rights conflict.

Falun Gong was founded by a man named Li Hongzhi in 1992. Li developed a set of physical and mental exercises that were meant to focus the human body's qi (the body's energy, according to traditional Chinese medicine). Li Hongzhi also developed elaborate spiritual, mystical teachings to go along with these breathing exercises. Li spoke of aliens walking among humans, and of discovering an ancient civilization on Earth that was connected to Falun Gong.

Li quickly developed a following among the Chinese people. The Chinese government had not authorized this group, and its rapid growth made Chinese leaders anxious. They began cracking down on Falun Gong activities and banned it completely on July 21, 1999. The group's teaching centers were shut down, and in the years since the crackdown, thousands of Falun Gong followers have been arrested, tried, and sent to prison. Many have died in prison from torture.

Meanwhile, outside of China, Falun Gong associations have been established in more than 100 countries. They regularly hold protest demonstrations, demanding that China free those who are being held in prison. Li Hongzhi, who was in the United States when the crackdown began, continues to live there.

■ These protesters are in Manila, in the Philippines, demonstrating in support of the Falun Gong.

THE RIGHT TO FREE EXPRESSION

Article 19 of the United Nations (UN) Declaration of Human Rights guarantees that everyone has the right to freedom of expression. This implies that anyone should be free to say anything to any audience. However, most people agree there should be appropriate limits on expression. The familiar question applies: "Is it wrong to cry 'Fire!' in a crowded theater if there is no fire?" This means that people should not say things that are intended to cause harm or false alarm. Also, making libelous statements (lies that damage another person) does not fall within the rights of expression. There are other kinds of speech that are banned by various countries.

More than two dozen countries have laws that ban various types of "hate speech." Hate speech can be described as an expression that is intended to incite hatred of groups based on their nationality, religion, race, religion, or sexual orientation. Germany and other European countries have laws that ban expressions of Holocaust denial. This is meant to stop people from spreading the idea that the Holocaust never happened.

WHAT DO YOU THINK?

How far should the freedom of expression extend? Should people be able to post any kind of information on websites? Who should decide what information should be censored?

Several countries have laws that do not allow the burning of flags. A flag is a symbol of a nation, and flag-burning is seen as an ultimate act of disrespect for the country. Denmark allows the burning of the Danish flag (because that is the traditional way of disposing of a flag), but it bans the burning of other nations' flags.

National security is another area where governments censor individuals' expression. People are banned from publishing confidential information about a nation's security forces that could potentially help the country's enemies. Deciding what is appropriate for the public to know and what must be kept secret, however, is a matter of debate. In 2010, a website called WikiLeaks began posting confidential U.S. military documents that exposed the inner workings of military operations in Iraq and Afghanistan. The U.S. government was upset by these postings, claiming that, by making the information public, national security was threatened.

■ Members of a group against the two-party political system in the United States burn an American flag in Boston, Massachusetts.

Internet censorship

The internet provides people with a vital connection to nearly any location or to any other computer user in the world. Still, millions of people do not have full access to the internet because their governments do not want them to have that access.

China, which has long censored news and entertainment media within its borders, has taken an aggressive stance against certain internet portals. While many of China's 1.3 billion citizens do have internet access, they cannot access Google, Facebook, or Twitter because these sites make it easy for people to find sites that might be critical of the Chinese government.

While China's internet censorship has focused on blocking content from entering China, other world leaders have blocked information from leaving their countries. For instance, when revolutions and wars flare up, some leaders attempt to stop the news media from covering these conflicts. In January 2011, revolutionary protests began to stir in Egypt against the reigning president, Hosni Mubarak. As thousands of anti-Mubarak protesters took to the streets, the Egyptian government blocked internet access in Egypt as a way of stopping the flow of information. As the *New York Times* reported, Egypt had somehow found an "off switch" for the internet. This development worried human rights advocates because of the assumption that the internet is immune from this kind of control. It is designed to work even if one part of the network goes down. So, people are now concerned that other governments could interfere with the information network if, or when, other crises emerge.

In the Information Age, access to the internet is beginning to be considered a basic human right.

THE RIGHT TO ACCESS

The present era has been called the Information Age. At no other time in human history has so much information been available to so many people, so quickly. The right to free expression is a basic human right, and, in our "wired" society, there does not seem to be any limit on the ways in which we can express ourselves.

In developing nations, however, technology is not necessarily free and is not necessarily available. Former UN Secretary General Kofi Annan has spoken about a "digital divide" that threatens poorer nations such as those in Africa, where fast, free access to the internet is not widely available.

Access to the internet is vital both as a way of allowing citizens to express themselves and as a way of breaking a cycle of poverty that drags down many nations.

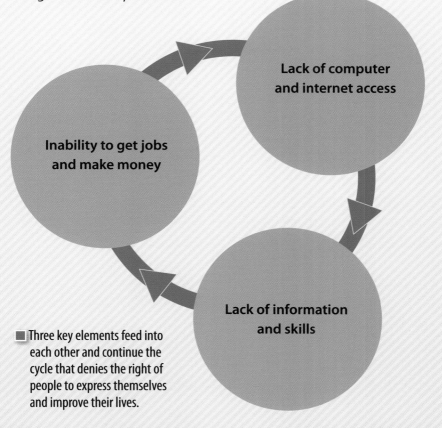

■ Three key elements feed into each other and continue the cycle that denies the right of people to express themselves and improve their lives.

Priorities of human rights

The UN list of 30 human rights spans a wide range of freedoms that we must work hard to protect. Some rights are matters of life and death. Other rights are not necessarily issues on which people's lives depend. A child's right to education is an important right, but a child's right to freedom from torture or murder are surely more important, or at least more urgent.

However, human rights may not be matters that we can prioritize. Rights are rights. We are born with rights, and no rights should be denied. Our rights are connected to each other. They make up a web of liberty that forms the basis of a free society.

CASE STUDY

Tank Man

In May 1989, the world saw some of the strongest protests against the government in China. Thousands of students demonstrated in Beijing's vast Tiananmen Square. The protests lasted several weeks before the government's military entered the square to confront the demonstrators and engage them in bloody battles. Today, it is still not known exactly how many lives were lost. The Chinese government says fewer than 300 were killed. Other experts put the death toll in the thousands.

On June 5, Tiananmen Square was still occupied by the army, and rows of tanks patrolled its perimeter. From a nearby hotel balcony, a foreign journalist was filming a line of at least a dozen tanks when, suddenly, a single man appeared on screen and ran in front of a tank. He was just an ordinary young man wearing a plain white shirt and black trousers, carrying a plastic shopping bag.

He stood in front of the massive tank, as if he were staring it down in a duel. Several more tanks rolled up behind the first, and the man stood there facing them. The front tank turned to drive around the man, but the man shuffled to his left to stay in front of it.

After several long moments, "Tank Man" (as he would eventually be nicknamed) climbed up the front of the lead tank and pounded on the hatch with his fist. He shouted into the tank and then climbed down and resumed his position. The confrontation continued for several more minutes. Finally, two men raced onto the scene, grabbed Tank Man, and hurried him out of view. To this day, nobody knows who he was or what happened to him.

Within a day, the film of this confrontation was broadcast around the world. Although it was not seen in China, it was seen throughout Europe, and in the ensuing months one communist regime after another was toppled by the revolt of the people. People involved in these revolts have said that the image of Tank Man emboldened them to persevere in their own revolutions.

In just a few minutes, this solitary man expressed more of the power and necessity of human rights than any law or declaration that has been written. He was one man, expressing himself. He acted alone, probably unaware that he was being filmed. He exercised the only freedom and power that he could muster at that moment. In a square where the military had just slaughtered thousands, one man threatened to bring peace by simply stopping, staring, and taking full advantage of his rights.

■ The showdown in June 1989 at Tiananmen Square in China inspired those fighting for human rights around the world.

THE UNITED NATIONS UNIVERSAL DECLARATION OF HUMAN RIGHTS

This list summarizes the rights explained in the 30 articles of the **United Nations** document, which was adopted on December 10, 1948. For the complete text of the declaration, visit **www.un.org/en/documents/udhr**

Article 1
All human beings are born free and equal.

Article 2
Everyone from all cultures, races, and genders is entitled to all the rights and freedoms set forth in this Declaration.

Article 3
Everyone has the right to life, liberty and security of person.

Article 4
No one shall be held in slavery.

Article 5
No one shall be subjected to torture or to cruel, inhuman, or degrading treatment or punishment.

Article 6
Everyone must be treated in the same way everywhere.

Article 7
Laws are the same for every person. Nobody should be treated with a different set of laws.

Article 8
If your rights have been denied, you should be able to get legal help.

Article 9
Nobody may be arrested and held in jail or deported without good reason.

Article 10
All trials should be done in public to make sure they are fair.

Article 11
Everyone charged with a crime will be presumed innocent until proved guilty according to law in a public trial. Everyone has the right to defend themselves at a trial.

Article 12
Everyone has the right to be protected if someone tries to harm them or invade their privacy.

Article 13
Everyone has the right to travel freely within their country. Everyone has the right to leave

and return to their home country.

Article 14
If harmed in their home country, everyone has the right to ask for asylum: protection in another country.

Article 15
Everyone has the right to a nationality: to be a citizen of a country.

Article 16
Adults have the right to marry whom they wish and to raise a family. Men and women have the same rights when they are married and when they are not married.

Article 17
Everyone has the right to own property, and nobody has the right to take it away without good reason.

Article 18
Everyone has the right to practice the religion they choose.

Article 19
Everyone has the right to think and say as they please.

Article 20
Everyone has the right to join groups and to have peaceful meetings of groups. Nobody can force another person to join a group.

Article 21
Everyone has the right to take part in the government of his or her country. Everyone has the right to vote, and all votes should be counted equally.

Article 22
Everyone has the right to the economic and cultural resources offered by their country.

Article 23
Everyone has the right to work, to choose their jobs, and to fair treatment by their employers. Men and women should receive equal pay for the same jobs. People should be free to create unions.

Article 24
Everyone has the right to rest and leisure and to take paid time off from work.

Article 25
Everyone has the right to earn a living so that they can afford food, clothing, housing, and access to social services that assist the elderly or ill. Mothers and their children should receive special care.

Article 26
Everyone has the right to free and equal education. Elementary education for children should be required. Parents have the right to choose the kind of education that shall be given to their children.

Article 27
Everyone has the right to freely participate in the cultural life (arts, sciences, traditions) of the community. Artists' and writers' work will be protected.

Article 28
Everyone should live in a social "order": an organized society in which everyone's rights are protected.

Article 29
Everyone is free to develop their own individual personalities; however, everyone also has duties to the community. Individuals may not infringe upon the rights and freedoms of other individuals.

Article 30
No person should act to destroy human rights.

GLOSSARY

advocate person who fights for or supports a position

ally person, group, or country that has joined with another for a particular purpose

amnesty pardon or forgiveness for any past crime or offense

apartheid system of laws in South Africa that separated people of different races and gave advantages to some races

boycott organized protest in which people stop buying certain products or using a company's services

burqa long garment worn by traditional Muslim women. A burqa covers the whole body, and includes a veil to cover the face.

chaos state of complete confusion; lack of order and rules

communist system of government that does not allow idividuals the right to own property, and rejects classes in society; supporter of communism

constitution document that describes the basic principles and rules of a country

democratic believing in social equality

developing country country in which the income is not yet high enough to ensure that most people have a high level of well-being

dictator ruler who has complete power over government and citizens

dissent disagreement; difference of opinion

dissident person who disagrees with a ruler or the government

domestic violence act of violence or abuse by one household member on another

execute put to death

genocide murder of a large number of people from a cultural, racial, or political group

Holocaust systematic mass slaughter of European Jews in Nazi concentration camps during World War II

Human Rights Watch independent organization that works to defend and protect human rights. It investigates and exposes human rights violations, and challenges governments and those who hold power to end abusive practices and respect international human rights law.

militia military force made up of civilians

parliament body of elected representatives who make the laws for a country

purge get rid of, exterminate

revolution fight that results in replacing the leader or the government that controls a country

Soviet Union 20th-century communist country of which today's Russia was a major part

surveillance watch kept over a person or group

UNICEF the United Nations Children's Fund, which works to protect the rights of children and young people worldwide

United Nations (UN) international organization comprised of many nations that enforces international law and provides aid to people and nations in need

violate break or disregard a law or rule

waterboarding a form of torture in which prisoners are submerged in water to make them feel as if they are drowning

FURTHER INFORMATION

Books

Downing, David. *Afghanistan* (Global Hot Spots). Chicago: Heinemann Library, 2004.

January, Brendan. *Genocide: Modern Crimes Against Humanity*. Minneapolis, Minn.: Twenty-First Century Books, 2006.

Lassieur, Allison. *Eleanor Roosevelt: Activist for Social Change*. Danbury, Conn.: Children's Press, 2007.

Robinson, Mary. *Every Human Has Rights: What You Need to Know about Your Human Rights*. Des Moines, Iowa: National Geographic, 2008.

Ross, Stewart. *The United Nations* (World Watch). Chicago: Heinemann Library, 2004.

Websites

Amnesty International's site focusing on issues related to children's rights
www.amnestyusa.org/our-work/issues/children-s-rights

Children's Rights
An organization that fights for children's rights
www.childrensrights.org

The Carter Center
President Jimmy Carter's organization, which advocates for voting rights and other human rights
www.cartercenter.org

Human Rights Watch
One of the world's leading human rights monitoring agencies
www.hrw.org

National Women's History Museum
Website with online articles and exhibitions tracing the history of the women's rights movement
www.nwhm.org

UNICEF
Website for the United Nations Children's Fund, a group that advocates for children's rights
www.unicef.org

United Nations Cyberschoolbus
The United Nations' educational site for kids
www.cyberschoolbus.un.org

Voices of Youth: Human Rights Page
A website run by UNICEF, with articles by and about young people
www.voicesofyouth.org/en/sections/human-rights

INDEX